"A serious call to commitment that will help all Americans understand and respond in times of crisis. A must read."
—**Captain Stanford E. Linzey, Jr.**
Chaplain Corps, U.S. Navy (Ret.)
Battle of Midway Survivor

"Chaplain Bohlman has addressed the reasons for our personal commitment and accountability to our Nation and to God in a very candid and practical way. Everyone who will serve in the U.S. Armed Forces should read *So Help Me God* before they take their military oath."
—**Joseph G. Gray, Major General, AUS (Ret.)**

"An inspiring book for all military members as well as civilians . . . everyone needs to be reminded of the founding principles of our country. For civilians, it will provide insights into the dedication of military members when they take the oath of enlistment. A great book with a lot of history, I highly recommend it."
—**Archie D. Sightler, Jr.**
Command Chief Master Sergeant
South Carolina Air National Guard (Ret.)

D1559734

SO HELP ME GOD

A Reflection on the
Military Oath

Brian Bohlman

Tulsa, Oklahoma

SO HELP ME GOD

So Help Me God by Brian Bohlman
Published by Insight Publishing Group
8801 S. Yale, Suite 410
Tulsa, OK 74137
918-493-1718

Unless otherwise noted, Scripture references are taken from the *Holy Bible: New International Version* ©. Copyright © 1973, 1978, 1984 by International Bible Society. Used by permission of Zondervan Publishing House. All rights reserved.

Cover Photograph: President Bush hosts reenlistment ceremony for 100 servicemembers at the White House, May 23, 2001. DoD photo by Staff Sgt. Scott Ash, U.S. Air Force (Released for public use). Display of U.S. Armed Forces seals does not constitute DoD endorsement of any nature; seals used with permission.

Copyright © 2003 by Brian Bohlman
All rights reserved.

ISBN: 1-930027-72-9
Library of Congress catalog card number: 2002112580

Printed in the United States of America

DEDICATION

To the proud and courageous men and women who presently serve or have served in the United States Armed Forces . . . thank you for your sacrificial and dedicated service to America at home and abroad. Your commitment to the military oath ensures the freedoms we enjoy today and reminds us that true freedom is never free.

Especially to all the "Swamp Foxes," whom I am privileged to serve alongside as "Rev" in peacetime and war.

May God help all those who serve to "bear true faith and allegiance" and may God always bless the United States of America.

BL Bohlman

PSALM 27:1-3

IN SPECIAL MEMORY

★ ★ ★ ★ ★

Firefighter Robert T. Bohlman, FDNY (Ret.)
March 18, 1916 – April 24, 2002

MSgt Ray A. Langston, USAF (Ret.)
April 15, 1921 – May 30, 2001

SMSgt Robert C. Fechner, USAF (Ret.)
April 4, 1934 – February 21, 2000

All casualties of the terrorist attacks
on America
September 11, 2001

All casualties of the War on Terrorism
. . . past, present, and future

They will never be forgotten

CONTENTS

FOREWORD

"I lift up my eyes to the hills — where does my help come from? My help comes from the Lord, the Maker of heaven and earth."
Psalm 121:1-2

The military oath ends as a prayer — as a cry out to the Almighty — "So help me God." It is entirely appropriate to begin upon such a note, because should the day come when you face the fire of combat, you will repeat those words, and more: "Help me God" "I need you God" "Deliver me God." After surviving the nightly bombings Iraq visited upon Northern Israel during the Gulf War, I came home to write about the experiences of those who had found their faith a firm foundation in time of battle. I interviewed many POW's from Vietnam, survivors of WWII and Korea and not one believed they made it through "by their own wits and skill."

One told me, "When I didn't know God, when I didn't want God, when I thought I didn't need God, He was still watching over me. I thought I was a smart man. I thought I was a strong man. But God showed me in Vietnam, no man is strong enough to save himself. I'm so grateful He did." (*Taking the High Ground: Military Moments with God*)

As you consider your responsibilities of the oath you take, consider also that it is God who is able to sustain and keep you in the hour of desperate prayers. You stand as one in the long line of men and women, who held everything from muskets to M-16's, who sailed the tall ships to carriers, who flew the biplanes to the spy planes and each of them faced their moments between breath and death. God will be there for you as He is for all who call upon His name.

I have found Christ sufficient for my darkest hours and most desperate prayers. As you commit yourself in service to this nation, may you also find comfort knowing the truth of the psalmist, "My help comes from the Lord."

Colonel Jeffrey O'Leary, USAF (Ret.)
Author of *Taking the High Ground*

PREFACE

September 11, 2001
One year later . . . and beyond

With the passing of the first anniversary of the September 11th terrorist attacks on America, our military forces remain committed in the global conflict against terrorism at home and abroad. As a result, the world is learning that the proud members of the U.S. Armed Forces are an elite and dedicated fighting force. **They are fighting in the War on Terrorism because each of them—as volunteers—took an oath "to support and defend (America) against all enemies, foreign and domestic . . . So help me God."**

Our military personnel need God's *help* more than ever as they confront those committed to our destruction. Without God's help, we will not prevail in the War on Terrorism. I am thankful that our Commander-in-Chief, President George W. Bush, and other national leaders have called on Americans to seek God's help, comfort, and strength in a post 9/11 world. As our military forces continue to wage war against terrorism, let us reflect on the words of a former U.S. president who served during an earlier crisis period in America: "Without the assistance of the Divine Being . . . I cannot succeed. With that assistance, I cannot fail."

Abraham Lincoln

Why read this book?

It is unfortunate that not much has been written or explained regarding commitment to the military oath. As a result, to some servicemembers, the oath is no more than a piece of paper filed away in their personnel record. Yet in reality, the oath is the legal document and commitment of honor that binds all servicemembers together as a fighting force that is ready and willing to preserve our God-given freedoms at all costs. Your military oath is much more than a piece of paper you signed.

As a first of its kind, this book is a valuable resource for reflecting upon your commitment to the military oath. As you read, you will discover the importance of drawing upon divine aid during your military service. The Appendix section contains helpful resources such as a list of common oaths and affirmations to reference when administering an oath, a compilation of the Core Values of the U.S. Armed Forces, and a copy of the Code of Conduct. In Appendix IV, I offer a helpful outline for conducting a "So help me God" Service of Reflection, which provides servicemembers an opportunity to reflect on the oath to which they subscribed.

It is my sincere hope and prayer that *So Help Me God* will become a helpful handbook for anyone who has taken the military oath in service of the U.S. Armed Forces. Please visit **www.SoHelpMeGod.org** to share your comments on the book and to find further help in fulfilling the commitment you made upon oath.

ACKNOWLEDGEMENTS

First and foremost, I want to thank my God for inspiring me to undertake this project. Throughout the entire process, He truly has been my Helper!

To my lovely wife, Shelley, whose prayers, sacrificial spirit, love, and support—as a military spouse and lifelong helpmate—allow me to focus on my calling and passion for military ministry. To my parents, Larry and Vicky, and brothers, Dan and Matt, whose never-ending prayers have sustained me in spirit, soul, and body.

To Rick and Tanya Curren, Marty and Kathy Davis, and Russ and Leah Shumard for their encouragement and guidance in the early days of the project. To everyone that took the time to offer feedback . . . you know who you are, and I sincerely appreciate your help.

To my editor, Tom Gilson, of Military Ministry: As a God-sent helper, Tom's expertise in manuscript editing and content evaluation is the reason this book became a reality. The men and women of the U.S.

Armed Forces can be thankful for his investment in this project.

To Dan Tindall of Net Designs Plus, Inc., for helping me link the "So Help Me God" Project to the world.

To John Mason, Scott Kaste, Adrienne Waner, and everyone else at Insight Publishing Group—thanks for your prayers and all the God-sent insights along the way.

An online "Wall of Honor" at www.SoHelpMeGod.org lists the names of individuals and organizations who contributed to the first printing of this book and the *So Help Me God for Servicemembers* outreach program.

One

"…So help me God."

*I encourage all to examine the words of the
Declaration of Independence and of the
Constitution, which together form the basis
for our freedom and prosperity. These documents serve as a constant reminder of the
oath that Congress has ordained for every
"individual elected or appointed to an office
of honor or profit in the civil service or uniformed services"*

The Honorable Donald H. Rumsfeld
Secretary of Defense
In Honor of Liberty Day, March 16th

. . . that I will support and defend the
Constitution of the United States against
all enemies, foreign and domestic; that I

will bear true faith and allegiance to the same; that I take this obligation freely, without any mental reservation or purpose of evasion; and that I will well and faithfully discharge the duties of the office on which I am about to enter. So help me God.

Inspired by Patriotism

Do you recall what you were doing on August 2, 1990? I was attending a special family gathering when the news reported the sudden invasion of Kuwait by Iraqi forces. I vividly recall watching the news on TV that evening and wondering if World War III was about to begin. From that day forward I stayed abreast of the mounting tensions in the Middle East and how America was responding to the crisis.

I remember the sudden call-up of National Guard and Reserve units in support of the newly named operation—Desert Shield. I recall listening to news stories about military personnel who were shocked about being activated and mobilized for possible combat. I distinctly remember seeing their faces on TV and listening to their personal stories—especially National Guard and Reserve troops from all walks of life—students, teachers, preachers, fathers, mothers, grandfathers, and grandmothers. Some were taken by surprise—many were speechless—obviously still in shock as I saw them pictured there on the news. All of them had known, however, when they volunteered to join the U.S. Armed Forces, that they could become activated and mobilized at anytime. They were also bound by military oath to "support and defend the Constitution of the United States against all enemies, foreign and domestic."

As I watched events unfold in the U.S. Armed Forces, I wondered if the draft would be reinstated. My mind raced as I thought about duty, honor, and Country. I thought about those of the "greatest generation," like my courageous grandfather who served with honor as an Army officer during World War II. I remembered my brave uncle who proudly served as a Navy fighter pilot in Vietnam and survived six treacherous years as a prisoner of war. I pondered the fact that freedom is never free, and that defending freedom is the responsibility of all Americans.

I knew that those who wore a uniform in the U.S. Armed Forces made a special commitment upon which our national freedom depended. As thousands of military personnel deployed to the Persian Gulf, I daily prayed that diplomacy might lead to a peaceful solution and that war would be averted.

When I returned to school in the fall of 1990, I had a hard time concentrating on my studies because I was preoccupied with the massive military buildup overseas. I became engrossed in the war of words between President George H. Bush and Iraqi President Saddam Hussein. It was hard to pull myself away from this drama as the words grew hotter and the final ultimatum was given to Saddam: "Get out now or you'll be forced out later!" We know "the rest of the story" and we're presently learning about the threat Iraq still poses in the present war against terrorism.

I share these personal reflections on the Gulf War because I want to express my deep gratitude to all veterans of foreign wars — but especially veterans of the Gulf War — and their families, friends, and civilian employers who supported them back on the home front. The sacrifice and commitment of Operation Desert Shield/Storm veterans inspired thousands of young Americans of my generation to join the U.S. Armed Forces. I became one of those thousands as I responded to the inner call to serve my God and Country in uniform when I enlisted in the early 1990s.

Understanding Commitment

In America today, true commitment and verbal integrity can be extremely hard to find. Commitments are broken every day. Just who can be trusted to keep their word? This is why, at certain crucial times, we ask people to take an oath. Among the paperwork that is required to enter the U.S. Armed Forces, there is a very important document called the "military oath."

It is a commitment to support and defend the Constitution of the United States of

America — something not to be taken lightly. The oath that all enlisted and officer personnel must recite upon entering the U.S. Armed Forces concludes with four of the most important words to be remembered throughout one's service to America: SO HELP ME GOD.

SO HELP ME GOD — The emphasis on "so" is demonstrated by the way this small word pulls together the entire oath, down to this final prayer-like phrase. The use of "so" may be thought of in the following manner: "Having taken into consideration all that I have repeated thus far, I now call upon Almighty God to help me fulfill my solemn commitment to the military oath." This understanding was certainly in the back of my mind as I stood before an officer and took my oath of enlistment at a military entrance processing station.

SO **HELP** ME GOD — The word "help" reveals exactly what should be requested at a special time of commitment. In the broad sense, "help" includes those divine resources, such as wisdom and strength, that are needed daily while serving in the U.S. Armed Forces. With each day I serve, I am constantly learning that God's help is often delivered in different forms and is experienced in and through His mysterious ways. Who would not want God's help as they officially enter the U.S. Armed Forces to support and defend (America) against all enemies?

SO HELP **ME** GOD—It is important to note that the oath doesn't read, "So help 'my country,' 'my commander,' 'my comrades,' . . ." Rather it is a *personal* request (So help *me* . . .) i.e., for God to specifically help the person taking the oath. It is not that you shouldn't ask God to help your commanders or comrades, but it is *your* signature on the military oath, not theirs. After subscribing to your oath, you become responsible for your actions and obligations as a member of the U.S. Armed Forces. You are no longer a "civilian" but a soldier, sailor, airman, Marine, or Coast Guard member.

SO HELP ME **GOD**—Again, note that it doesn't read, "So help me 'man upstairs,' 'higher power,' 'abiding force,' . . ." Rather, it calls on the ultimate Helper by name—God! Historically, this reference to God has most often been understood to be the Almighty

God, revealed to us in the Holy Scriptures, upon which U.S. presidents and other government officials have placed their left hand while taking the oath of office. So, as you look to God—who has helped guide men and women throughout wars and national disasters—you join with those who entered into the service of the U.S. Government or Armed Forces by calling upon God for help on one of the most important days of their lives.

America's first President and Commander-in-Chief, George Washington, took his oath of office with his left hand upon a Bible opened to the book of Deuteronomy, Chapter 28. He then gave his famous "Inaugural Speech to Both Houses of Congress," in which he stated: "It would be peculiarly improper to omit, in this first official act, my fervent supplications to that Almighty Being who rules over the universe, who presides in the councils of nations, and whose *providential aids* can supply every human defect."[1]

Two

A Reflection on the
Military Oath

*If we ignore the historical importance of our
profession, the society from which it comes, and
why it is worth preserving, we run the risk of
the guardians not valuing what they guard.*

General John A. Wickham, USA (Ret.)
30th Chief of Staff
United States Army

*"So help me God" symbolically cements the
seal of personal commitment—a commitment so sincere that we are prepared to lay
down our lives to support and defend our
Constitution.*

Major General Clifford L. Stanley, USMC
Deputy Commanding General

Live by using the lessons of the past as a reference to aid your journey into the future.

Michael P. Green
Spiritual leader and Author

Many of America's Founding Fathers believed in Almighty God. These leaders sought Divine favor and blessing, and acknowledged the work of Providence upon this great Nation.[1] On April 30, 1789, America's first Commander-in-Chief, President George Washington, concluded his presidential oath of office (see Appendix I) by adding four words to form a most fitting and prayerful plea: SO HELP ME GOD. With the addition of "So help me God," Washington set a historical precedent that other U.S. presidents have since followed. During the Revolutionary War, the "So help me God" phrase became part of official military oaths. Since then millions of American servicemen and women have proudly raised their right hand, repeated their military oath, and concluded by calling upon God to help them fulfill an awesome commitment to bear "true faith and allegiance" to the Constitution and to the United States of America. There are different versions of the military oath depending on duty status (active, reserve, or national guard), and rank (enlisted or officer). However, all oaths for military personnel conclude with the phrase, "So help me God."

A Call for Solemnity

Subscribing to the military oath is a very serious matter. The moral stability of a society hinges on the sanctity of an oath. By taking an oath, a person promises to abide by his or her *word and obligations* even as God is faithful to His word. People can invoke divine judgment and the curse of the law upon themselves if they fail to uphold their oaths. Taking the oath is much more than a historic ritual required by the law. Though outwardly, you stand at attention beside an American flag with your right hand raised before a commissioned military officer, inwardly, your heart should swell with pride as you are administered the military oath. Commenting on the administration of the military oath, Major General Clifford L. Stanley (USMC) said:

No exceptions are made when it comes to repeating this oath. Everyone in the military has said it and in most cases will have cause to say these words again, or at the very least witness an occasion when someone else will say them. Before beginning their journey to basic training, all servicemembers recite the same oath—officers a slightly different version than enlisted. "*So help me God*" symbolically cements the seal of personal commitment—a commitment so sincere that we are prepared to lay down our lives to support and defend our Constitution. The words of our oath leave no room for situational ethics. Twenty-four hours a day, 7 days a week, and 365 days a year—we're always on duty. We're also held to a very high standard of ethical conduct, and our actions, be they positive or negative, "always" reflect on our Nation and the uniform we wear.[2]

In a world where some believe there are no absolutes, this thought-provoking statement reminds us of the absolute seriousness that must accompany the commitment to the military oath.

Why Oaths?

Imagine how wars could be fought and won if servicemembers were not bound by a compelling commitment to support and defend the Constitution of the United States? An oath is a form of a loyalty test, in that one swears or affirms to be faithful and committed to fulfill an obligation or attest to the truth. Military members take an oath because they are entrusted with the awesome duty of defending America "against all enemies, foreign and domestic." Since the terrorist attacks on September 11, 2001, more Americans are aware of our need for a strong national defense. The military oath is the legal document that requires servicemembers to obey the orders of the president, a governor of a state, and the officers appointed over them. The Uniform Code of Military Justice enforces this commitment.

Military members are not the only persons required to take an oath. Judges are sworn in before walking into the courtroom. Before a witness may testify, a judge will ask them to raise their right hand and will place them under the following oath or one similar to it: "Do you swear that the testimony you are about to give will be the truth, the whole truth, and nothing but the truth, so help you God?" The person responds by saying, "I do." To lie under oath is perjury, a severe criminal offense.

Physicians, who have the power of life and death, have traditionally taken the Hippocratic oath. Lawyers, appointed, and elected officials come under oath before entering into their official office. Immigrants who wish to become naturalized citizens take an "Oath of Allegiance" which requires them to "bear arms on behalf of the United States when required by the law" or "perform noncombatant service in the Armed Forces of the United States when required by the law." Refer to Appendix I for a list of the common oaths and affirmations of the United States.

What is an Oath?

When examining an oath, it is important to consider how the original framers of the military oath understood an "oath" in their day. Webster's earliest edition of *An American Dictionary of the English Language* defines an oath as:

> A solemn affirmation or declaration, *made with an appeal to God* for the truth of what is affirmed. The appeal to God in an oath, implies that the person imprecates his vengeance and renounces his favor if the declaration is false, or if the declaration is a promise, the person invokes the vengeance of God if he should fail to fulfill it. A false oath is called perjury.[3] (emphasis mine)

Unfortunately, some modern dictionaries have removed or reworded the moral and religious components of an oath. This is contrary to the way some of our Founding Fathers understood an oath. John Adams, our second president, admonished American military officers that "Oaths in this country are as yet universally considered as sacred obligations."[4]

Sacredness of an Oath

As a military chaplain, I am concerned with the spiritual health of U.S. Armed Forces personnel. I view oath-taking as a solemn and sacred act with clear implications. When I first took the military oath upon my enlistment and later when commissioned, I looked far above myself—to the ultimate Judge and Helper—for wisdom, strength, and courage in fulfilling my sworn commitment to God and Country.

In Greek, *herkos*, translated as "oath" in English, is "a fence, an enclosure, that which restrains a person; a guarantee of the discharge of liabilities." In Latin, *sacramentum*, translated "sacrament" in English "is a sacred symbol or token, e.g., the oath of allegiance taken by Roman soldiers; hence, a sacred ceremony used to impress an obligation; a solemn oath-taking."[5]

From a biblical perspective, an oath is a holy ritual, and to swear falsely is to profane God's name.[6] Swearing by God's name was most solemn, but people also swore by holy things, and by raising their right hand.[7] Covenant ceremonies demanded the swearing of oaths. The apostle Paul swore by an oath, and even God has bound himself by an oath.[8] Understanding the sacredness of an oath should cause us to consider the consequences of not living up to our promises. Whenever we are tempted to give up or give in, that is when we need God's help more than ever. With God's help, "mission impossible" can become "mission possible."

One Nation Under God

On June 26, 2002, the Ninth U.S. Circuit Court of Appeals ruled that the Pledge of Allegiance to the U.S. Flag cannot be recited in public schools because the phrase "under God" endorses religion. The court ruled that reciting this phrase is a violation of the alleged Constitutional separation of church and state. This controversial ruling has outraged the majority of Americans of faith who declare, along with the Founding Fathers, that our rights to life, liberty, and the pursuit of happiness come from God. As this book goes into publication, this ruling is in the process of being challenged. Interestingly, George

Washington faced similar attacks in his day against the sacred heritage of oaths.

Washington took his oath seriously and felt very strongly about its meaning. In his famous Farewell Address, he expressed his dismay over the skepticism, agnosticism, Deism, and atheism creeping in from France and the French Revolution. He believed these philosophies could destroy the faith behind the oaths and undercut the security of society.[9] In fact, Washington said,

> And let us *with caution* indulge the supposition, that morality can be maintained *without* religion. Whatever may be conceded to the influence of refined education on minds of peculiar structure, reason and experience both forbid us to expect, that national morality can prevail *in exclusion of* religious principle.[10] (emphasis mine)

Despite the prophetic warnings of Washington over two centuries ago, some have sought to remove the name of "God" from all oaths and from the swearing in of witnesses in court. However, if this occurs, it would appear that they would no longer be bound *by God* to fulfill the constitutional requirements of the office or the law. They would solemnly swear or affirm *by themselves*, seemingly escaping accountability to the highest Authority. As a result, if a law would seem disagreeable to them, or if they regard their own ideas as superior, it would be all too easy for them to decide that it was acceptable to circumvent the law. In essence, they would become their own judge and jury; a final authority unto themselves.

Consequently, where there is no regard for truth or when people can subscribe to oaths and vows with no intention of abiding by their terms, then social anarchy and degeneration ensue. Where there is no fear of God, then the sanctity of oaths and vows disappears, and people begin to shift the foundations of society from the truth to a lie.[11]

Constitutionality of "So help me God"

Regarding the constitutionality of the phrase, "So help me God," the following was recently published in a set of historical documents relating to the duty of all who serve within the Department of Defense to honor and to uphold the law:

It might appear to some that Congress requiring every "elected or appointed to an office of honor or profit in the civil service or uniformed services" to take an oath of office concluding with "So help me God" (5 U.S.C., Section 3331) would violate the First Amendment's prohibition against "an establishment of religion." To the contrary, oaths *have always* been an essential element of our constitutional system. In his 1796 Farewell Address, President George Washington described the fundamentally religious nature of oaths: "Of all the dispositions and habits which lead to national prosperity, Religion and morality are indispensable supports . . . [W]here is the security for property, for reputation, for life, if the sense of religious obligation *desert* the Oaths, which are the instruments of investigation in Courts of Justice?"[12]

Though there have been several revisions to the military oath of office over the years, the "So help me God" phrase has remained intact.

So Help Me God — A Daily Prayer

As a member of the U.S. Armed Forces, you have volunteered to become part of something much bigger than yourself. In doing so, you have made an awesome commitment to support and defend the sacred values and principles in our Constitution. The fact is that our local, state, national, and international defenses are only as strong as our commitment to the military oath. When you publicly acknowledge God and ask Him to help you fulfill your military oath, you have repeated one of the most unselfish and humble prayers known to man.

This prayer-within-an-oath is a great way to begin a military career. God wants us to ask Him for help not just once, however, but every day. How it must hurt our Creator to watch His children live their lives without asking for His help. One of the most effective prayers we can pray is simply: "Please, help me, God!" Through this simple prayer, we acknowledge our inability to succeed by our own unaided efforts and we declare our dependence upon God for help. I believe that if you continue to ask God for help, He will help you to "bear true faith and allegiance" in fulfilling your solemn commitment to the military oath. I have personally experienced amazing answers to this daily prayer.

When Taking the Oath

From time to time, I have the honor and privilege of administering the military oath to new recruits and those re-enlisting. Participating in this special event reminds me to reflect upon my commitment to "bear true faith and allegiance" and live by those last four words of our oath. On the one hand, there is an indescribable pride and humility that comes over me when I administer the oath to a military member. On the other hand, I am disappointed that some military members have not carefully read or don't take the time to consider their commitment to the military oath. How can a military member be ready to fight and willing to die for a commitment they don't understand or fully accept?

Your military oath must be upheld and respected from the day you place your signature under it. Your oath should be a source of pride and patriotism during your service to America in peacetime and war. Read your military oath often and make it a habit to ask for God's help on a daily basis. As you read this book, know that my sincere hope and prayer is that you will become more informed about the military oath and will seek the ever-present help of God. In conclusion, it is fitting to quote Major General Stanley's summation on this subject:

> The oath—did we really mean it? Did we understand what we were saying when we said, "*So help me God*?" If we all did, our jobs would be easier—no more court-martials, no small unit level disciplinary problems, and no concern over popular interpretation over the orders and laws we have sworn to uphold. Active interpretation of our oath, passionate commitment to service, and gen-

uine love of *our Nation and our God* are the mortar that holds our sworn commitment together. All who wear our Nation's uniforms should be the beacons of all that's good and right about America.[13] (emphasis mine)

My Challenge to You

To those proudly serving in the U.S. Armed Forces: Never forget that your military oath is a serious commitment to yourself, your family, your unit, your State, your Nation—and most importantly—your God. You have already asked God to help you on one of the most important days of your life. My challenge to you is that you will continue to ask for God's help at anytime, in any place. God loves you and is your ever-present help in trouble.

Three

An Ever-Present Help in Trouble

O God, our help in ages past,
our hope for years to come,
Our shelter from the stormy blast,
and our eternal home!

Isaac Watts, Hymn writer (1674-1748)
Based on Psalm 90

Fear not, I am with thee; O be not dismayed,
for I am thy God, and will still give thee aid;
I'll strengthen thee, help thee, and cause thee to
stand, Upheld by My righteous, omnipotent hand.

"How Firm a Foundation:"
Traditional Hymn, c. 1787

*Yesterday, December 7, 1941 — a date which will live in infamy — the United States of America was suddenly and deliberately attacked by naval and air forces of the Empire of Japan . . . With confidence in our armed forces, with the unbounding determination of our people, we will gain the inevitable triumph, **so help us God!***

President Franklin D. Roosevelt
Address to the Nation
December 8, 1941

On September the 11th, enemies of freedom committed an act of war against our country. Americans have known wars — but for the past 136 years, they have been wars on foreign soil, except for one Sunday in 1941. Americans have known the casualties of war — but not at the center of a great city on a peaceful morning. Americans have known surprise attacks — but never before on thousands of civilians. All of this was brought upon us in a single day — and night fell on a different world, a world where freedom itself is under attack . . . Great harm has been done to us. We have suffered great loss. And in our grief and anger we have found our mission and our moment. Freedom and fear are at war.

The advance of human freedom — the great achievement of our time and the great hope of every time — now depends on us. Our nation — his generation — will lift a dark threat of violence from our people and our future. We will not tire, we will not falter, and we will not fail.

President George W. Bush
Address to the Nation
September 20, 2001

God's help often comes to us in unsuspected forms. If you've ever told someone about a difficult situation you're facing, perhaps they've replied by saying, "God is able to work out all things for good." While that's true in the long run, it doesn't always help to hear that at the moment. Yet, I once heard a story that illustrated how God was able to bring a blessing out of what appeared to be a curse.

Many years ago, a terrible storm arose in the Atlantic Ocean and broke apart a large fishing vessel. Only one crew member survived by holding onto a piece of wood and washing up on a nearby uninhabited island. He mourned the loss of his friends and felt guilty that he was the sole survivor. Though he didn't understand why God had allowed his life to be spared, he believed God had a special plan for him and prayed daily for His help. A week later, while he was searching for food, a lightning storm suddenly appeared over the island. As he made his way back to the shelter he had built, he noticed a large column of smoke. As he ran over to it, he discovered his hut and all his supplies in flames. Now, not only was he alone, but everything he had gathered to help him survive, had burned up!

That night he fell into a deep depression and questioned whether God still had a plan for his life. In the morning, he walked down to the shore to find some food. To his amazement, he looked up to see a ship lying offshore and a small boat rowing toward him. As soon as he met the men in the boat, he asked them how they knew he was in trouble. They replied, "We saw your smoke signal yesterday but because of the storm, we had to wait until now to come get you." [1]

Like many of us, this shipwrecked man's first action was to cry out to God for help. Yet, not everyone responds in this way. While helping people in crisis, I've seen some people run away from God and His help, while others run directly to Him. It is unfortunate that some people do not seek God's help until they are in desperate need, because God wants to help us all the time. God's help is always available, but perhaps we feel unworthy of it, too proud to ask for it, or reject it altogether.

Lesson on Accepting Help

Perhaps you've heard the familiar story about the man who climbs to the roof of his house during a sudden storm surge. As the waters quickly rise, he prays to God for deliverance. Within moments, a rescue worker spots him on his roof and swims over and offers to help him get to dry ground. However, the man refuses, explaining he is waiting for God's help. The waters continue to rise. A little while later someone in a lifeboat pulls alongside his house and offers to take him to safety, but the man remains on the roof, declaring he is awaiting a sign from God. The water now covers over the neighbor's house and is beginning to touch the lower portion of his roof.

Shortly thereafter, a helicopter hovers above the house and lowers a rescue line as the water reaches the tip of his roof. Still the man waves the helicopter away and shouts back, "My God will help me!" As the helicopter flies away, the man becomes engulfed in the waters. As he fights to stay afloat, he cries out to God, "My God, why haven't you helped me?" A voice from heaven replies, "I sent you a rescue worker, a boat, and a helicopter, but you refused them all. What more did you expect Me to do?"

This story illustrates how God's help often comes in ways that we may not expect. Sometimes the help we seek is much closer than we think. Though miracles and divine intervention still occur, God often works behind the scenes through our circumstance. For example, God's help may come through a sympathetic friend or coworker to talk to, an unread book, or the members of a place of worship. When in a painful situation, it is tempting to shut yourself off from others—even those who truly care for you. When you are confronted by troubling circumstances, God is still with you. He has promised never to leave you nor forsake you.[2] Although you may feel as if God is not there, He is. It reminds me of the thought-provoking lyrics to a song I once heard:

Sometimes He calms the storm with a whisper, "Peace be still." He can settle any sea but it doesn't mean He will. Sometimes He holds us close and lets the wind and waves go wild. Sometimes He calms the storm and other times He calms His child.[3]

Your Way vs. God's Way

There is a way that seems right to a man, but in the end it leads to death.[4] Do you want to live life God's way, according to His direction? Most people do, but it's much easier said than done. As a military member, your ultimate source of authority is derived from God.[5] Behind the authority of your military rank or badge is military law, state and federal law, and ultimately God's law. With the authority entrusted to you comes great responsibility.

God wants to be a part of your decision making process. People of faith seek God's help by asking for divine wisdom, strength, and courage each day. It is implied that when you asked God for help in your oath, that you wanted help in doing things *His* way—not your way. Yet, this is not always the case. When you said, "So help me God" as you concluded your military oath, did that mean, "God help me to do things *my* way" or "God help me to do things *Your* way"? There is a world of difference between your ways and God's ways.

We often view our life events from an earthly perspective, but God has the ultimate "big picture" from a heavenly perspective. Imagine if you had to put together a massive puzzle without having the picture on the box to use as a guide. You may discover how a few of the pieces fit together, but it would become a long, frustrating process—especially working by yourself.

Yet, this is exactly how life can be when you face situations and choose to go it alone rather than asking for God's help along the way. Wouldn't it be easier to have faith and trust God instead of trying to figure out how the pieces of your puzzle fit together on your own? This has been my challenge in life. Yet along the way, I have learned how to discover God's nearness in times of despair.

Discover God's Footprints in Your Life

The thought-provoking and inspirational poem titled "Footprints" has brought comfort to many people who have felt alone or distanced from God during a difficult season in their life. It is the story of someone who, looking back on the "path" of their life along the sand, saw two sets of footprints—their own and God's. At the worst times of their life, though, there was only one set of footprints, and they asked, "God, why did You desert me at those hardest times?" To which God replied, "At those times, my child, I was carrying you."

I suggest you start to discover God's footprints in your life, even right now. Pause for a moment and take an inventory of your life by reflecting on the following question: At what point(s) have you sensed that God was carrying you through the dangerous minefields and battlefields of life? God promises to draw near us as we draw near to Him.[6] It may take years after a stressful event or tragedy to see God's help—His footprints—in a circumstance you've faced. Sometimes you may never understand "why," but that doesn't mean that God has forsaken you. My belief is that there will always be some painful situations in life that we will never fully understand on this side of eternity. If we try to explain the unexplainable by filling in the blanks where God seems to be absent, we are guilty of tampering with the mysterious ways and sacred silence through which the sovereign God of the universe works.

Wherever you are in your faith journey, remember that God is with you in the valleys of doubt as well as the mountaintops of joy. As you stop and ask God for help, I hope you'll discover His holy footprints in your life, both past, present, and future.

In God We Trust

While I am extremely proud of America's military might and capabilities, I am also aware of how such pride can lead to placing our *sole* hope and trust in our manpower and might, rather than in the God we claim to trust. God forbid—as members of the greatest fighting force in the world—we place our sole hope and trust in something or someone other than Almighty God. America has a rich heritage of faith and has been extremely blessed by God. If America will bless God, God will bless America. However, we can forfeit those blessings by becoming a nation that trusts only in self, status, or stuff rather than in God.

How true is the proverb that warns us that "pride comes before a fall."[7] Along the same thought, the psalmist instructs us in saying, "Some trust in chariots and some in horses, but we *trust in the name* of the LORD our God."[8] The following stories of faith and courage are about people who saw their need for God's help and placed their trust in Him.

Pearl Harbor Reflections

On Sunday, December 7, 1941, Gordon "Gus" Gustafson, a sailor aboard the USS Battleship Tennessee in Pearl Harbor, Hawaii, was engaged in a prayer meeting with another Christian sailor, Hervy Vendrick, just prior to the Chapel Service on the quarterdeck. His personal reflection of the "Day of Infamy" follows:

We were moored just forward of the Arizona and inboard of the West Virginia, with the Maryland and Oklahoma just forward of us. About 7:55 a.m. a frantic call to "General Quarters! General Quarters!" broke up our prayer meeting. Sudden bomb blasts convinced us it wasn't a drill! As we ran to our respective battle stations, I told my friend, "If I don't see you down here, I'll see you up there," referring to heaven.

I helped carry a wounded sailor through our compartment, followed by responding to the P.A. system call to "Man number two motor launch on the double!" Rushing topside I was greeted by intense fire and smoke from the sunken Arizona, where 1,177 men were already swept into eternity. That was the only order I never followed as the number two motor launch was a ball of flames and I wasn't going to commit suicide!

At that point I really didn't have time to pray — apart from "shooting up" a quick request for help. Later, when there was a lull in the action and I was locked in a watertight compartment with several other men, I opened my Gideon New Testament with Psalms and Proverbs. Immediately, my eyes fell on the words in Psalm 3:4-6: "I cried unto the Lord [for help] . . . and He heard me . . ." My shipmates appreciated the fact that I had freedom and assurance to call upon God in that desperate moment.

The rest of that "Day of Infamy" was spent fighting fires and asking God to help men trapped in the sunken ships around us. The next day I witnessed the rescue of men pulled out of the capsized

Oklahoma and spent the rest of the day pulling out oil-soaked bodies from the water.[9]

Four Brave Chaplains

Commitment always involves sacrifice. No one understands this better than those who have laid down their lives so that others may live. This was true of the four Army chaplains aboard a troop transport ship on its way to Greenland during World War II. The following account, written by Victor M. Parachin, illustrates the unselfishness, dedication, and bravery of four chaplains who made the ultimate sacrifice. As you serve America, reflect on their commitment to duty, honor, and Country.

On the evening of Feb. 2, 1943, the troop transport ship Dorchester was crowded to capacity, carrying 902 servicemen, merchant seamen, and civilian workers across the North Atlantic from Newfoundland to an American base in Greenland. The ship's captain was anxious about German U-boats in that area, ominously dubbed "Torpedo Junction." Earlier that day, in fact, a Coast Guard cutter escorting the Dorchester detected an enemy submarine nearby. So even though the vessel was just 150 miles from its destination, the Dorchester's captain ordered the cramped crew to be prepared and to sleep in their clothing and lifejackets.

His fear was all too justified. Just before 1AM., a German submarine spotted the hulking ship and fired a torpedo. Struck on the starboard side, the old coastal liner quickly began sinking into the 36-degree water. Scores of the mostly young men were wounded or killed. Others, panicked, leapt into overcrowded lifeboats while several rafts drifted away, empty. The cutters could only rescue 227 survivors.

It took only 27 minutes for the ship to go down. But throughout these horrifying moments, four chaplains showed extraordinary bravery: Army Chaplains Lt. George L. Fox (Methodist); Lt. Alexander D. Goode (Jewish); Lt. John P.

Washington (Roman Catholic); and Lt. Clark V. Poling (Dutch Reformed).

These four chaplains fanned out to calm the frightened, tend to the wounded, and guide the disoriented toward safety. They distributed lifejackets, and when those ran out, gave away their own. As the ship went down, survivors floating in nearby rafts could see the four heroic chaplains — arms linked and braced against the slanting deck, offering final prayers into the chilling wind. Said one of the survivors, "It was the finest thing I have ever seen this side of heaven."[10]

I believe that the following conclusions can be made about the sacrificial spirit and commitment of these four courageous chaplains:

- They became "visible reminders of the Holy" as they provided help to others in need.
- They remained calm and preached courage and strength in the midst of total chaos.

- They comforted each other and those around them as they prepared to meet their Maker.
- They united across religious boundaries to serve all of God's people in need.

A Prisoner of War in the "Hanoi Hilton"

Robinson Risner was shot down on a bombing mission over North Vietnam. During his seven and a half years in Hoa Lo Prison, more infamously known as the "Hanoi Hilton," Risner was subjected to the most brutal tortures and suffered almost every imaginable deprivation as his captors tried to break him and use him for propaganda. His endurance through this trial by fire revealed how the smartest and bravest rely on their faith in God and our American way of life. After returning from Vietnam, he continued to serve in the United States Air Force and later retired as a Brigadier General.[11]

A Rescued Pilot Returns with Honor

On June 2, 1995, U.S. Air Force Captain Scott O'Grady was helping enforce the

NATO no-fly zone in the skies over Bosnia when an anti-aircraft missile tore into his F-16. As his jet began to explode, he ejected from his aircraft at five miles up while traveling 350 miles per hour. As he descended into the hostile territory of war-torn Bosnia, he called upon God for help like never before. After he spent six difficult days and nights evading the enemy, the U.S. Marines made a daring and successful daylight rescue mission. O'Grady relied upon his survival training and deep faith in God to evade and escape his enemies.[12] All in all, he exemplified Article VI of the Code of Conduct of the U.S. Armed Forces (reference Appendix III).

A Miraculous Landing

In April 2001, a U.S. Navy surveillance plane made a remarkable and miraculous landing on China's Hainan Island. According to news sources, a Chinese F-8 fighter jet challenged and collided with a U.S. Navy EP-3 spy plane on a routine mission. After losing part of the wing and nose of the aircraft, the courageous pilot,

Lieutenant Shane Osborn, wrestled to regain control of the plane as it plummeted eight thousand feet and made an emergency landing. After being harassed, interrogated, and detained for eleven days, the twenty-four-member American crew was released. Upon their jubilant return to the United States, Lieutenant Osborn and the other crew members publicly acknowledged the awesome help of God in safely landing the plane and sustaining their spirits. The crew also testified to their deep faith in God, the miraculous power of prayer, and the strength they received from singing spiritual songs in captivity.[13]

Reflect on Your "So help me God" Stories

These are just a few of the "So help me God" stories that illustrate the ever-present help of God during challenging times. If you reflect on your military service, you most likely will discover the helping hand of God at work behind the scenes. Recall your "God moments" and remember His faithfulness to you when facing the challenges that are a part of military life.

In reality, we will all face trouble in life, but with God's help, we can better cope with the challenges to commitment.

Four

Coping with Challenges
to Commitment

*There are, it may be, many months of **fiery trial** and **sacrifice** ahead of us . . . To such a task we can **dedicate** our lives and our fortunes, everything that we are and everything that we have, with the pride of those who know that the day will come when America is privileged to spend her blood and her might for the **principles** that gave her birth and happiness and the peace which she has treasured. **God helping her**, she can do no other.*

President Woodrow Wilson
War Message, 1917

Our Servicemen and women are serving throughout the world as guardians of peace —

*many of them away from their homes, their friends, and their families. They are **visible evidence** of our determination to meet any threat to the peace with measured strength and high resolve. They are also evidence of a harsh but inescapable truth — that the **survival of freedom** requires **great cost** and **commitment**, and great **personal sacrifice**.*

President John F. Kennedy
Armed Forces Day, 1963

*No President has ever had reason to doubt the **ability** and **commitment** of the American Armed Forces. You have shown that **commitment** today . . . The choice was yours to make, and you volunteered again, and your country is **very grateful**. Our military **depends on re-enlistment** . . . Perhaps more than ever, the success of our **all-volunteer force** requires that we keep the best people, the most experienced technicians, and mature leaders of the highest caliber. That is what America gains with each one of you who stays. For those who are about to take the oath, congratulations. You repeat some familiar words. You will do so with self-assurance that you might not have* *done the first time. That comes with **hard work** and **discipline** and **service** to our country. I want each of you to return to your posts with the knowledge that you have my **gratitude** and **full confidence**. Thank you again.*

President George W. Bush
Military Re-enlistment Ceremony
The White House, May 23, 2001

As the global fight to root out terrorism enlarges, there will be significant losses on all sides of the conflict. Americans should be reminded often that all servicemembers and their families make daily sacrifices for the sake of preserving freedom. Service in the U.S. Armed Forces is based on a unique commitment that will include challenges far beyond what your civilian compatriots will normally face. As you consider all of the challenges to keeping your commitment to serve, you may often ponder the following question: How can I really live up to what I promised in my oath?

A Test of Commitment and Love

My commitment to the military oath was challenged when I was a young airman.

Shortly after returning from a winter deployment, I asked for my girlfriend's hand in marriage—and she said "Yes!" Over the next few months, Shelley and I attended premarital counseling and made plans for a beautiful summer wedding and honeymoon. About five weeks before our wedding day, we spent an evening preparing all of our invitations to be mailed the next day. When I arrived to work the following morning my supervisor called me into his office to talk about an important phone call he had received.

For the next few moments I sat stunned as I learned that higher headquarters had just "selected" me to deploy to a secret location for six months . . . and I needed to report for duty *in one week*! You can imagine the betrayal and anger I felt. "How could this happen *to me*? Doesn't the military care that I have plans to get married next month? This must be a mistake!" How was I going to explain this to Shelley? As I left the office, I said a quick prayer for God to help me calmly process the situation as I drove to her workplace.

While in the car, God reminded me of the commitment I made when I took the military oath to "support and defend" and "bear true faith and allegiance." God also reminded me that He would be there to help me fulfill my sworn commitment. Though things didn't seem "fair," my Country had called upon me to serve somewhere in the world, and I had to be there in a week. As I reflected on my commitment to serve, I recalled that there was no special provision in the military oath that exempted service "for those about to be married."

Over lunch I told Shelley about the short-notice deployment orders I'd received and she, too, was very disappointed and upset. Yet, from the time she said "Yes" to my proposal, she had understood the commitment and the potential sacrifices of being married to a military member. After asking God for wisdom and speaking to our families, we decided to get married immediately. We had a beautiful chapel wedding and a quick honeymoon. As events unfolded, my deployment was delayed for another four weeks. Ironically, I reported for duty in Guantánamo Bay, Cuba on the day before my original wedding date in July. Over the next three months, Shelley and I shared our love through letters, phone calls, audio and videotapes that we made for each other. With God's help, we made it through this unexpected period of separation, and as a result, our commitment to love was strengthened.

More Challenges to Commitment

You can imagine how challenging it is to receive a short-notice deployment order a month before you are to be married. Chances are, you have a story of your own challenges to military life. Yet, this is exactly the type of military that we voluntarily joined when we took our oath. I know my story is not that uncommon in a day when the average military member is deployed sometimes three or more months out of every fifteen.

Just remember that God is there to help you make it *through* the challenges, rather than get *out* of them. You can probably relate to some of the following challenges to your own commitment:

■ Family separations (missing birthdays, anniversaries, holidays, babies' births . . .)

- Deployment hardships (longer tours, more rotations, living in "field conditions" . . .)
- Difficulty connecting with a support system (problems at home, within the unit . . .)
- Danger (increase of terrorism, unwelcome presence in foreign lands, "friendly" fire . . .)
- Hard work, long hours, low pay, little recognition (lack of support for veterans . . .)

You need to take these challenges seriously. Just as it is impossible for a building to stand without supporting beams and girders, it is extremely difficult for military members and their families to stand up under these pressures when not all of their "support beams" are in place.

An Oath of a Military Spouse

Since a civilian spouse of a military member does not take a military oath, it is almost as if they are "drafted" into the military through marriage. Often the toughest job in the military is being the spouse of a military member. Shelley certainly would agree during times of separation when she remains alone to run the household. As a result, she came up with the following version of an oath for the spouse of a military member.

An Oath of a Military Spouse

I, _____, wife (or husband) of military member _____, do solemnly swear (or affirm) that I will support and encourage my military member as he (or she) fights against all enemies, foreign and domestic; that I will bear true faith and allegiance to the same; and that I will obey the orders of the military no matter when or where it takes my military member, that I take this obligation freely, without any mental reservation or purpose of evading my commitment to my military member; and that I will well and faithfully discharge the duties of a military spouse. So, help me, help me, God!

This "oath" highlights the unwavering commitment of the civilian spouse who works tirelessly behind the scenes so that their military member can support and defend them against all enemies. Without a doubt, I would have never received my commission, completed seminary, entered the chaplaincy, and founded the "So Help Me God" Project without the prayers, sacrifices, love, and support from my lifelong lover and helpmate, Shelley.

During the long hours of study and work, Shelley was always there to pick me up when I wanted to give up. I will always be eternally grateful for her. Due to my military reserve summer tours of duty, we were separated during our anniversary and her birthday during the first six years of our marriage. Thankfully, Shelley discovered a support system within the military environment that could help make our separations more bearable. However, she had to be willing to utilize the resources available to her.

The most crucial thing she learned was to ultimately lean on God's help as she looked for other forms of help available to her. The same is true for you and your loved ones. There are family, spiritual, unit, community, and national resources to help you, though I could not possibly list them all in this book. However, I've posted some suggestions and links on my web site at www.SoHelpMeGod.org. The web site is an excellent companion to this book and also contains "So help me God" stories that will inspire faith and courage as you serve. As long as there are enemies of freedom, foreign and domestic, there will always be significant challenges to your commitment in the military.

A Personal Challenge

> *Trust in the LORD with all your heart, and lean not on your own understanding; In all your ways acknowledge Him, and He will make your paths straight.*
>
> Proverbs 3:5-6

As I wrote this book, I often paused to consider those who would be reading these words. In reality, I have no idea *who* you are or *where* you are in your life as you read this—but God does! You may be going through a painful divorce, grieving the loss of a close friend or family member, dealing with an addiction, or overwhelmed by financial problems. Maybe you're a Private First Class on a plane heading out on your first overseas deployment or a Petty Officer who just shipped out for six months of sea duty. Possibly, you're a newly promoted Lieutenant Colonel who has just been assigned to command a squadron of fighter aircraft or a new Staff Sergeant who has just been given the responsibility for supervising a platoon of young Marines.

On the one hand, some of you may be on orders for a one-year remote duty assignment, while on the other hand, others may be attending enlisted basic training, technical school, officer training school, or a military academy. Still others may be recently separated or retired from the U.S. Armed Forces. Although I cannot know your exact situation, God does and He promised to be your ever-present help in time of trouble. *In what areas of your life do you need His help today?*

Pause for a moment and think back to the day you stood before an officer and took your military oath for the first time. I'm sure you were just as scared as I was when standing among a group of young people at a military entrance processing station who had just signed their life away to the U.S. Armed Forces! My friend, it is important to remember that you concluded your oath by calling upon God to help you fulfill an awesome commitment you made to yourself, your family, your unit, your state, your Nation, and your God. Since you've asked God to help you before, nothing should keep you from asking Him again.

One way you can ask God for help is through prayer. Prayer is simply a mode of personal communication with God. Scripture records that after King Solomon had prayed and dedicated the temple in Jerusalem, God said, "If My people, who are called by My name, will humble themselves *and pray* and seek My face and turn from their wicked ways, then I will hear from heaven and will forgive their sin and heal their land."[1]

We are in great need of God's forgiveness, healing, and help. We have all sinned and forsaken God's greatest commandments "to love the Lord your God with all our heart, and with all our soul, and with all our mind" and "to love our neighbor as ourself."[2] When you ask God for help, you acknowledge your total *dependence upon Him*. This is not a sign of weakness but rather a sign of strength, courage, and faith!

We live at a time when secular humanism is a popular system of belief. Secular humanism is a philosophy based on the nature, interests, and ideals *of man* and believes that man is capable of self-fulfillment and ethical conduct outside of God. Despite the plethora of "self-help" and "how-to" books available today, these cannot provide long-lasting help to problems that require a spiritual solution. That is why we should not rely solely on self, but on God for help.

I challenge you to ask for God's help in *every* area of your life: personal, family, spiritual, vocational, professional, etc. My prayer is that you will take time to reflect on your oath, apply the principles discussed in this book, and continue to ask for God's help, at anytime, in anyplace. For your spir-

itual growth and encouragement, please
visit www.SoHelpMeGod.org often.

Thank you for serving America in our
great armed forces. May God help and bless
you with every spiritual blessing as you face
the unique challenges of bearing "true faith
and allegiance" in the Armed Forces of the
United States of America. Godspeed.

9/11/01
We Will Never Forget

Since "9/11," we have all heard about the extraordinary faith and courage of those who perished trying to help others on that tragic day. I am personally inspired by the billboards around the nation that depict core values such as "courage," "sacrifice," and "commitment" with images of the military personnel, police officers, firefighters, medical workers, and other heroes who responded to the rescue efforts at the World Trade Center and Pentagon. As one billboard aptly stated, "When others ran out, they ran in."

As long as I live, I will never forget the events of September 11, 2001, nor should any American—especially those serving in the U.S. Armed Forces. President George W. Bush continues to remind all Americans that the War on Terrorism will be long-lasting and costly. As we have learned in past conflicts, and again since Operations Noble Eagle and Enduring Freedom began, true commitment involves sacrifice. Military members and their families may better understand the personal sacrifices they will make as they reflect on the sacrifice of innocent civilians killed on September 11, 2001.

From Fear to Faith

Just as December 7, 1941, became a "day of infamy" in American history, may September 11, 2001, be remembered as a day when Americans found strength in their faith, family, freedom, and flag to rise above the evil that was intended to bring us to our knees in fear. In reality, the tragic events of 9/11 have rallied Americans behind our men and women in uniform as they strive to root out terrorism at home and abroad. Yet, our struggle is far from over. So, please remember to pray for our fellow servicemembers who volunteered to sup-

port and defend us against all enemies . . .
So help them, and us, Almighty God, Amen.

Common Oaths and Affirmations of the United States

President of the United States [1]

I, _____, do solemnly swear (or affirm) that I will faithfully execute the office of the President of the United States, and will to the best of my ability, preserve, protect and defend the Constitution of the United States. *So help me God.*[2]

U.S. Representative, Senator, and Other Elected or Appointed Official [3]

I, _____, do solemnly swear (or affirm) that I will support and defend the Constitution of the United States against all enemies, foreign and domestic; that I will bear true faith and allegiance to the same; that I take this obligation freely, without any mental reservation or purpose of evasion, and that I will well and faithfully discharge the duties of the office on which I am about to enter. So help me God.

Active Duty or Reserve Officer of the U.S. Armed Forces [4]

I, _____, (SSN), having been appointed a (rank, category), United States (branch of service), do solemnly swear (or affirm) that I will support and defend the Constitution of the United States against all enemies, foreign and domestic; that I will bear true faith and allegiance to the same; that I take this obligation freely, without any mental reservation or purpose of evasion; and that I will well and faithfully discharge the duties of the office upon which I am about to enter, so help me God.

National Guard Officer
of the U.S. Armed Forces [5]

I, _____, (SSN), do solemnly swear (or affirm) that I will support and defend the Constitution of the United States and the Constitution of the State (Commonwealth, District, Territory) of _____ against all enemies, foreign and domestic; that I will bear true faith and allegiance to the same; and that I will obey the orders of the President of the United States and of the Governor of the State (Commonwealth, District, Territory) of _____, that I take this obligation freely, without any mental reservation or purpose of evasion; and that I will well and faithfully discharge the duties of the Office (Grade), in the Army/Air National Guard of the State (Commonwealth, District, Territory) of _____ upon which I am about to enter, so help me God.

Active Duty or Reserve Enlisted Member of the U.S. Armed Forces [6]

I, _____, do solemnly swear (or affirm) that I will support and defend the Constitution of the United States against all enemies, foreign and domestic; that I will bear true faith and allegiance to the same; and that I will obey the orders of the President of the United States and the orders of the officers appointed over me, according to regulations and the Uniform Code of Military Justice. So help me God.

National Guard Enlisted Member
of the U.S. Armed Forces [7]

I, _____, do solemnly swear (or affirm) that I will support and defend the Constitution of the United States and the Constitution of the State (Commonwealth, District, Territory) of _____ against all enemies, foreign and domestic; that I will bear true faith and allegiance to the same; and that I will obey the orders of the President of the United States and of the Governor of the State (Commonwealth, District, Territory) of _____ and the orders of the officers appointed over me, according to law and regulations, so help me God.

Oath of Allegiance for U.S. Citizenship [8]

I hereby declare, on oath, that I absolutely and entirely renounce and abjure all allegiance and fidelity to any foreign prince, potentate, state or sovereignty, of whom or which I have heretofore been a subject or citizen; that I will support and defend the Constitution and laws of the United States of America against all enemies, foreign and domestic; that I will bear true faith and allegiance to the same; that I will bear arms on behalf of the United States when required by the law; that I will perform noncombatant service in the Armed Forces of the United States when required by the law; that I will perform work of national importance under civilian direction when required by the law; and that I take this obligation freely without any mental reservation or purpose of evasion; so help me God.

Core Values of the
U.S. Armed Forces'

Importance of Core values

At the foundation of each branch of service in the U.S. Military lie core values that every service member should embrace as his or her own during their service to America and beyond. Core values provide guidance and direction to military members and help them build character that will be tested under fire. The following list of Core Values has been compiled from official web sites of the U.S. Armed Forces:

UNITED STATES ARMY

**Loyalty, Duty, Respect, Selfless Service,
Honor, Integrity, Personal Courage**

*Values are at the core of everything our Army is
and does. Your commitment to living and teaching the Army's core values is critical to our success today and tomorrow.*

General Dennis J. Reimer, USA (Ret.)
33rd Chief of Staff
United States Army

UNITED STATES NAVY

Honor, Courage, Commitment

Our core values . . . enrich our Sailors, our society, and our Navy's readiness. That is why we believe so strongly in character development, first instilling these values in basic training and then constantly reinforcing them throughout a Sailor's career.

Vice Admiral Alfred G. Harms, Jr., USN
Chief of Naval Education and Training
United States Navy

UNITED STATES AIR FORCE

Integrity First, Service Before Self,
Excellence In All We Do

Our core values, Integrity first, Service before self, and Excellence in all we do, set the common standard for conduct across the Air Force. These values inspire the trust which provides the unbreakable bond that unifies the force. We must practice them ourselves and expect no less from those with whom we serve.

General Michael E. Ryan, USAF (Ret.)
16th Chief of Staff
United States Air Force

UNITED STATES MARINE CORPS

Honor, Courage, Commitment

Semper Fidelis . . . the Marine's pledge to remain always faithful to these values and to God, Family, Country, Corps. Our core values remain the very soul of our institution, underlying all that is best in Marines, and continue to frame the way we live and act as Marines.

General Charles C. Krulak, USMC (Ret.)
31st Commandant
United States Marine Corps

UNITED STATES COAST GUARD

Honor, Respect, Devotion to Duty

We will transform our Coast Guard to meet the demands of the 21st century, confident in the enduring character of our service and strengthened by the core values of honor, respect and devotion to duty.

Admiral Thomas H. Collins, USCG
22nd Commandant
United States Coast Guard

Code of Conduct of the U.S. Armed Forces [1]

I

I am an American, fighting in the forces
which guard my country and our way of life.
I am prepared to give my life in their defense.

II

I will never surrender of my own free will.
If in command, I will never surrender
the members of my command while they
still have the means to resist.

III

If I am captured I will continue to resist by
all means available. I will make every effort
to escape and to aid others to escape.
I will accept neither parole nor special
favors from the enemy.

IV

If I become a prisoner of war, I will keep
faith with my fellow prisoners. I will give
no information or take part in any action
which might be harmful to my comrades.
If I am senior, I will take command.
If not, I will obey the lawful orders
of those appointed over me and will back
them up in every way.

V

When questioned, should I become a prisoner
of war, I am required to give name, rank,
service number, and date of birth. I will evade
answering further questions to the utmost of
my ability. I will make no oral or written
statements disloyal to my country and its
allies or harmful to their cause.

VI

I will never forget that I am an American,
fighting for freedom, responsible for my
actions, and dedicated to the principles
which made my country free.
I will trust in my God and in the United
States of America.

"So help me God"
Service of Reflection [1]

The following is a suggested order of service for conducting a "So help me God" Service of Reflection. Share this page with your chaplain and commander to discuss how such a service could be provided at your location. Perhaps offering a special service on Memorial Day weekend or in conjunction with July 4th events or Veterans Day functions in November would be fitting.

Since September 11, 2001, we need to offer more opportunities in our military communities to reflect on God, Country, and the oath to which we subscribed. In this way, we remind ourselves of the awesome commitment we made to support and defend this great Nation, with God's help!

"So help me God" Service of Reflection
Our Commitment to Support and Defend

Prelude
Instrumental Patriotic Medley

Presenting the Colors
Military Honor Guard

National Anthem
Military Member (Soloist)

Pledge of Allegiance
Commander

Posting the Color
Military Honor Guard

Invocation
Chaplain

Opening Song
Sung by Assembly
*(Choose patriotic songs like America the Beautiful,
My Country 'Tis of Thee, . . .)*

Responsive Reading (from Scripture)
Military Member

Patriotic Reflection
Military Member (Guest Speaker)
(The speaker should direct his/her remarks on how God specifically helped them fulfill their oath during their service to America. Speaker could be an active, guard/reserve, or retired military member.)

Renewing Our Oaths
(All enlisted members will stand, raise their right hand, and recite their oath of enlistment as administered by an officer. Then a senior ranking officer will ask all officers to stand, and administer the oath of office in a similar manner.)

Oath of Enlistment
Military Officer

Oath of Office
Military Officer

Closing Song
Sung by Assembly
(Choose patriotic songs like God Bless America, Branch of Service Hymn, . . .)

Benediction
Chaplain

Postlude
Instrumental Patriotic Medley

About the
"So help me God" Project

The "So Help Me God" Project is a faith-based organization for the preservation of core values within the U.S. Armed Forces. Our goal is to equip servicemembers with spiritual resources that will reinforce character, inspire faith in God, and preserve core values. Our vision is to encourage service-members to seek God's help everyday as they serve in the armed forces.

Please visit our web site at **www.SoHelpMeGod.org** to learn more about the resources we offer.

<u>**Note**</u>: **Discounts available for bulk purchases of** *So Help Me God*, **see web site for details.**

Wanted: Your "So help me God" Story

We want to hear from you! If you have a story that would encourage and inspire someone serving in the U.S. Armed Forces, we invite you to share it with us. Submission guidelines are available on our web site or by writing us at the address below. If selected, your story could appear on our web site or in our follow-up book: *So Help Me God Stories: A Reflection on Faith and Courage in the U.S. Armed Forces.*

The "So Help Me God" Project
PO Box 280662
Columbia, SC 29228

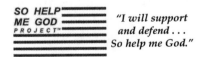

SO HELP
ME GOD
PROJECT™

*"I will support
and defend . . .
So help me God."*

About the Author

Chaplain Brian L. Bohlman has more than ten years of enlisted and commissioned service in the U.S. Armed Forces. He and his wife, Shelley, are the directors of the "So Help Me God" Project, a faith-based organization founded for the preservation of core values within the U.S. Armed Forces.

He is a member of the U.S. Air Force Chaplain Service and has served on active duty as a chaplain assistant and in the reserves as a chaplain candidate. He is presently a chaplain assigned to the 169th Fighter Wing, McEntire Air National Guard Station, Eastover, South Carolina. He has served in the following military operations: Bright Star, Northern Edge, Sea Signal, and Noble Eagle.

He is an ordained minister endorsed by the Chaplaincy of Full Gospel Churches of Dallas, Texas, an affiliate of the Military Ministry of Campus Crusade for Christ, an associate member of Officers' Christian Fellowship, and a member of the Military Chaplains Association.

His civilian chaplaincy experience includes ministry in a hospital trauma center, Life Flight, and prison ministries. He also frequently volunteers his ministry services to police and fire departments, as well as civilian businesses. He received his ministry training and degrees from Liberty University and Columbia International University.

Chaplain Bohlman and his wife, Shelley, reside in Lexington, South Carolina.

If he can be of service to you or your organization, please contact him at:

Chaplain Brian L. Bohlman
"So Help Me God" Project, Inc.
PO Box 280662
Columbia, SC 29228

Fax: 803-356-7568
Internet: www.SoHelpMeGod.org
E-mail: Brian.Bohlman@SoHelpMeGod.org

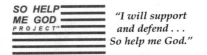

"I will support and defend . . . So help me God."

ENDNOTES

Chapter 1

[1] April 30, 1789, President George Washington's Inaugural Address. James D. Richardson, *A Compilation of the Messages and Papers of the Presidents*, 1789-1897 (Published by the Authority of Congress, 1899), Vol. 1, pp. 52-53.

Chapter 2

[1] For an encyclopedia of quotations from the Founding Fathers, see William J. Federer, *America's God and Country* (Coppell, TX: Fame Publishing, 1994).

[2] Maj Gen Clifford L. Stanley, "So Help Me God". . . Did You Mean It?, *Marine Corps Gazette*, Vol. 84, No. 8 (August 2000): 37.

[3] Noah Webster, *An American Dictionary of the English Language,* 1828 ed. (San Francisco, CA: Foundation for American Christian Education, 1987).

[4] Introduction (page "i") of SECDEF "Abridged Compilation of Constitution," taken from http://www.defenselink.mil/pubs/liberty.pdf

[5] W.E. Vine; Merrill F. Unger, et al, *Vine's Expository Dictionary of Biblical Words* (Nashville, TN: Thomas Nelson Publishers, 1985), p. 438.

[6] See Exodus 20:7; Leviticus 19:12.

[7] See Deuteronomy 6:13; Matthew 5:36; 23:16-22; 26:63; Revelation 10:5-6.

[8] See Genesis 26:28; 2 Corinthians 1:23; Galatians 1:20; Hebrews 6:13-18.

[9] See R.J. Rushdooney, *The Institutes of Biblical Law* (Phillipsburg, NJ: Presbyterian and Reformed Publishing, 1973), 111-112

[10] James D. Richardson, *A Compilation of the Messages and Papers of the Presidents, 1789-1897* (Published by the Authority of Congress, 1899), Vol. 1, p. 220.

[11] See Rushdooney, 115, for a thought-provoking commentary on oaths and modern society.

[12] Introduction (page "i") SECDEF "Abridged Compilation of Constitution," taken from http://www.defenselink.mil/pubs/liberty.pdf

[13] Maj Gen Stanley, 37.

Chapter 3

[1] Adapted from Michael P. Green, *Illustrations for Biblical Preaching*, electronic edition, 1989.

[2] Hebrews 13:5-6 ; Psalm 23

[3] Tony Wood and Kevin Stokes, lyrics to "Sometimes He Calms the Storm," BMG Music, 1995.

[4] Proverbs 14:12

[5] Romans 13:1-7

[6] James 4:8

[7] Proverbs 11:2

[8] Psalm 20:7, emphasis mine.

[9] Adapted from Gordon Gustafson, *Pearl Harbor Reflections*, self-published tract, 2001. Used with permission.

[10] Victor M. Parachin, "Four Brave Chaplains." Courtesy of http://www.fourchaplains.org. Used with permission.

[11] See Robinson Risner. *The Passing of the Night*. Ballantine Books, 1973.

[12] See Scott O'Grady. *Return with Honor*. Doubleday Publishing, 1995.

[13] See Shane Osborn. *Born to Fly*. Broadway Books, 2001.

Chapter 4
[1] 2 Chronicles 7:14, emphasis mine.

[2] Matthew 22:37-39

Appendix I
[1] Authority: United States Constitution, Article 2., Section 1., Paragraph 7 requires that this oath or affirmation be taken before a president enters into the execution of the office.

[2] When George Washington added the phrase "so help me God" to his presidential oath on April 30, 1789, he set a historical precedent that other U.S. presidents have followed by acknowledging the sovereignty of God over the affairs of nations. It is also customary for an incoming president or other elected official to take an oath with their right hand raised and their left hand placed on a Bible. This historic tradition is in no

way contrary to the provisions of the first amendment to the Constitution, for a distinction must be made between the existence of religion as an institution and the belief in the sovereignty of God. To ask for the assistance of the Almighty on one's first day in office is altogether proper and fitting in a Nation whose motto is: "In God we trust."

[3] This oath is mandated by Article VI of the Constitution and its text is set by statute (5 U.S.C., Sec. 3331).When appointed or elected to an office of honor and trust under the Government of the United States, a person is required to take and subscribe to the Oath of Office as prescribed by law before entering upon the duties of the office. The same is true of some city, county, and State employees but is governed by individual States.The same applies to the oaths or affirmations required by the Constitution and prescribed by law to be taken and subscribed by each Senator, in open Senate, before entering upon their duties. (5 U.S.C., Sec. 3331).

[4] Authority: 5 U.S.C. 3331, Oath of Office. Depending on the Branch of service, slight variations in may occur. For example, commissioned officers in the U.S. Air Force also state their

Social Security Number, the rank in which being appointed to and category, if appropriate, and the Branch of military service. Source: AF Form 133, Mar 1992.Example: "I, John Doe Smith, 123-45-6789, having been appointed a First Lieutenant, Chaplain, United States Air Force, do solemnly . . ."

[5] Authority: Title 32, U.S.C. Section 308 and 312, and Executive Order 9397. Source: NGB Form 337, May 1999.

[6] When enlisting in a Branch of Service in the United States Armed Forces, a person is required to take and subscribe to the Oath of Enlistment as prescribed by law. Authority: 10 U.S.C., Section 502, Title 10: Armed Forces, Subtitle A: General Military Law, Part II: Personnel, Chapter 31: Enlistments. This oath may be taken before any commissioned officer of any armed force. Source: DD Form 4/2, Jan 2001.

[7] DD Form 4/2, Jan 2001 also contains the oath of enlistment in Item 16 for National Guard (Army or Air) enlistees.

[8] See http://www.ins.usdoj.gov/graphics/ aboutins history/articles/OATH.htm for information on taking the Oath of Allegiance when becoming a U.S. citizen.

Appendix II
[1] Quotations and references to core values located on official web sites of the U.S. Armed Forces.

Appendix III
[1] Code of Conduct of the U.S. Armed Forces reprinted from *Survival, Evasion, and Recovery* manual, June 1999, page v. Approved for public release.

Appendix IV
[1] Permission granted to copy "So help me God" Service of Reflection pages; provide credit to Brian L. Bohlman, *So Help Me God: A Reflection on the Military Oath*, Tulsa, OK: Insight Publishing Group, 2002. http://www.SoHelpMeGod.org.

To our men and women in uniform . . .
past, present, and future:
God bless and thank you for serving in the
U.S. Armed Forces.

To:_____

*"God is our refuge and strength,
an ever-present help in trouble.
Therefore we will not fear..."*
— Psalm 46:1-2

From:_____

(U.S. Navy photo by Michael W. Pendergrass)

I pledge allegiance to the Flag of the United
States of America and to the Republic for which
it stands: **one Nation under God,** Indivisible,
with Liberty and Justice for All.

What others are saying about *So Help Me God . . .*

"The So Help Me God Project of Chaplain Brian Bohlman and his wife, Shelley, is a timely and cogent effort. We must have God's help and blessing to succeed as persons and as a Nation. All of our Founding Fathers knew this as do all worthwhile patriots ever since. I heartily endorse this project and book."
—**Chaplain, Colonel, E.H. Jim Ammerman**
U.S. Army (Ret.)

"Most people are longing to live life meaningfully, to give themselves to some cause greater than any one person. Brian Bohlman has demonstrated that service in the military is a worthwhile and noble life mission, and, as with life, a mission too large to handle without the help of God."
—**William Evans, Ph.D.**
Assistant Professor of Counseling Psychology
James Madison University

"Not today, not tomorrow, not ever, will our land, America, be without God's love. Prepare yourself well to defend, honor, and commit to God and Country with pride. This book is a bullet."
—**Commander Ralph E. Gaither**
U.S. Navy (Ret.) Ex-POW, Vietnam